PROGRAM MANAGEMENT ANALYTICS

PROGRAM MANAGEMENT ANALYTICS

BHARAT GERA

In memory of the little one ...

CONTENTS

Introduction

Any project executed in today's marketplace, whether a gaming project launch in Las Vegas, Nevada, USA; a healthcare project in Beijing, China; a government policy project in the Philippines; or a space launch project at NASA is based on strong analytic foundations. Today, mankind is at a flux of high technology to harness any information source or intelligence, including our own Mother Nature to gain deeper insights into process behavior and patterns that include in-built uncertainties.

Uncertainty in processes cannot be neglected, and a predictive approach is the rule of the day. The CEOs, CIOs, are CTOs of today no longer accept uncertainty as the "ignore" factor in making decisions. As a project manager, I no longer report the estimated project schedule or cost with definitive numbers and make a disclaimer of project risks. Traditional project management envisages and supports the legacy paradigm. Today, project managers need to report the project metrics in terms of "analytic certainty" as Project X has:

- *Schedule of 3PW (person weeks) + 0.5 PW with a 95% confidence interval*
- *Cost of US$3000 + US$100 with a 99% confidence interval*

Am I asking statisticians to be project managers? Not really! Rather, I propose the basics of statistical analytics, which can be learned by tenth-grade students and incorporated in A Guide to the Project Management Body of Knowledge (PMBOK® Guide)—Fourth edition (PMI, 2008).

Before I detail the enhancements to the project management principles (as per the PMBOK® Guide), I briefly introduce the required analytical concepts.

PART 1

Business Analytic Theory

Analytic Concepts - Basics

*Numerical measures of processes and systems have an inherent characteristic to follow **probability distributions** determined by the underlying process type e.g. process measure relying on independent accumulated data values. This essentially means that, any numerical measure of the system is bound to occur a certain number of times if the system process is repeated in the long term.*

E.g. Project X is expected to hit 24 risks in the 1 year schedule. Assuming a Poisson Risk Process, the project should be geared to close 73% of the risks within a 20 day period per risk.

The above example is a demonstration of how analytical results can be practically applied in project executions. Do not worry about the example calculations, we will understand them further in the sections to follow.

Common Probability Distributions observed in Project Management Scenarios (PMBOK® Guide)

In this note, we are going to consider some common analytical probability distributions that we encounter frequently in project settings. The distributions are "analytical" because they are the product of analyses that mathematicians and statisticians have performed on the nature of the underlying processes that give rise to them (they conducted these analyses precisely because the processes are frequently encountered.) The advantage of having these distributions is that once we determine they are appropriate for a given situation, we can both more accurately represent the uncertainty we face (in building a project risk model, for example) and frequently gain important insight into a situation with much less effort.

*We must determine which analytical distribution to use for a given problem. **The metrics of uncertainty is captured in a probability distribution**. There are two major methods we can use: The first method compares the processes that generate the data; the second compares the data distributions themselves. In the first approach, we must define the process that is generating the experienced uncertainty/variation and compare it to those that are known to generate particular analytical distributions. In the second approach, we generate a frequency distribution from historical data and compare it directly to known analytical probability distributions. The second method is the philosophy behind "best fit." Software packages. If we find a significantly close match between our distribution and a particular analytical distribution, we can assume that the underlying process must be of the type that produces that particular analytical distribution....even if we do not have a precise definition of the process itself*

Uniform Distribution

We start with perhaps the simplest of distributions in terms of underlying process. If
every value in a range has an equally likely chance of being generated by a process, then a uniform distribution accurately describes the likelihood of getting individual outcomes. The parameters of a uniform distribution are simply its minimum and maximum value; all values within this range are possible. Because this is a continuous distribution, it is not meaningful to talk about the chance of getting one specific outcome; for example, the chance of current project schedule being exactly 9 month and 1 day is too small to be seriously contemplated. Thus, as with all continuous probability distributions, we can only meaningfully talk about the chance of getting outcomes within ranges. It is easy to calculate the probability of any specific range of outcomes in a uniform distribution, as it is simply the ratio of the specific range to the total range of the distribution. For example, if the minimum is 0 and the maximum is 10, the probability of getting a value between 0 and 4 is simply 4/10 = .40, where 4 is the size of the specific range and 10 is the size of the overall range.

A uniform distribution is appropriate when you do not believe any value within a range of possible outcomes is more likely than any other. It is often associated with having very little knowledge about outcomes beyond being able to specify a range. A downside of using this distribution is that outcomes at the extremes of the range are just as likely as outcomes in the middle; even with little knowledge, people often recognize that this is unlikely. That having been said, the uniform distribution is often considered conservative because it spreads out uncertainty as broadly as possible within the range.

Normal Distribution (A Fundamental Aggregation Distribution Observed in Nature)

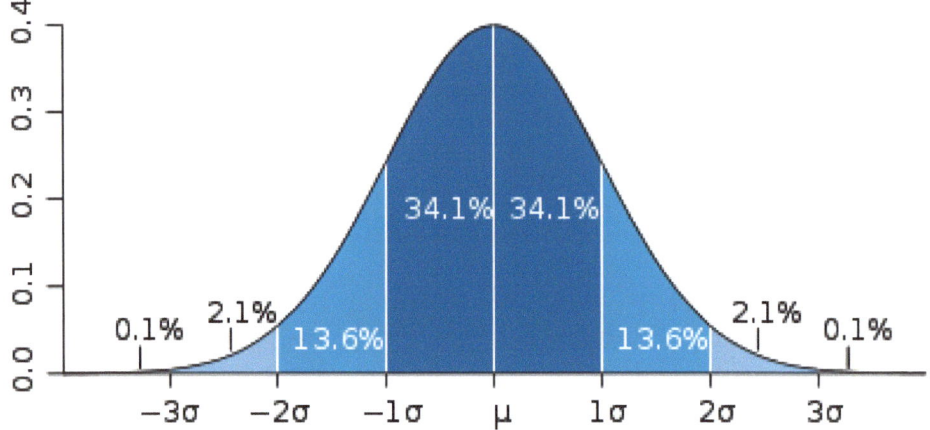

Figure 1: Normal distribution.

*The familiar bell-shaped curve of the normal distribution is undoubtedly the most recognizable of all probability distributions. It is also the most frequently misused. While many processes in project management (as described in **PMBOK® Guide**) and organizational management/business do give rise to normal distributions, it is by no means ubiquitous. **The underlying process that gives rise to a normal distribution is an accumulation process.** Whenever an outcome is really the sum (or average) of the outcomes of a number of uncertain quantities, different or the same, the probability distribution of the outcome is frequently a normal distribution. In fact, one of the most famous theorems in statistics, the central limit theorem, implies this directly: If you have enough uncertain quantities going into the accumulation, the resulting distribution of the sum (or average) will be normal.*

For example, organizations base their performance system on this distribution where employee appraisal naturally falls into an average 360 feedback / accumulation mechanism. This will leave the organization with fixed percentages of employees in the high, medium and low brackets.

Also, the height of females of a certain race is normally distributed (but not the height of all people of the race, which will have two spikes or modes, one centered on the average height of men, the other of women). Many industrial machines that produce products with certain target specifications (for example, holes with a diameter of 20 centimeters) will actually produce outcomes that vary slightly around the target (slightly more or less than 20 centimeters) due to the precision limits of the equipment. The distribution of deviations is often normal. Stock market portfolios, comprised of multiple stocks, produce accumulated period returns that are normally distributed. In the stock market example, it is clear what, "accumulation." is taking place: that of the returns on the individual stocks. For the other two examples, it is not so clear what is being accumulated. Data on female heights of a given race, however, unequivocally establish that the result is a normal distribution, as do data on the variation from specifications for many industrial machines. We assume that there must exist some kind of underlying accumulation taking place (body parts? lots of small perturbations that influence the actual size of the diameter?) that produces the normal distribution of outcomes we observe.

Unfortunately, because we observe the normal distribution so frequently in the world, and yet often cannot identify the underlying accumulation process that produces it, it is easy to fall into the trap of assuming every distribution is normal. In general, we should only be willing to accept normality if (1) we have a clear understanding of the underlying accumulation process that is occurring (such as with the return on stock market portfolios or more generally in sampling situations) or (2) we have sufficient data on previous outcomes to convince us that a normal probability distribution is appropriate.

*How do we determine if data supports the assumption of normality? To answer this, it is useful to recognize some important characteristics of normal distributions. First, the two parameters of a normal distribution are the mean and standard deviation. "Standard deviation." is simply one of several ways to measure how dispersed actual outcomes are likely to be from the mean of a distribution. The formula for the standard deviation of a set of data (**x**1, **x**2, **x**3, …. **xn**) is,*

$$\mathrm{sqrt} \left(\frac{(x_1 - X)^2 + (x_2 - X)^2 + (x_3 - X)^2 + \ldots + (x_n - X)^2}{n} \right)$$

*where "sqrt" is "square root" **X** is the mean of the data and **n** is the number of data. Standard deviation can be thought of as stating the **average** difference between a given outcome and the mean. But if standard deviation can be thought of as simply this average difference, why are we squaring and taking square roots? Why not just take the absolute value of the actual difference between each datum and the mean and the average of that? In general, the answer is: If all we are interested in is some measure of dispersion, there is no reason to prefer one to the other (except you might prefer the latter because it is more straightforward!). BUT, when the distribution is normal, the standard deviation turns out to be an enormously valuable thing to know, as we shall soon see.*

As parameters, the mean and standard deviation define a particular instance of a normal distribution. In the introduction, we cited two such instances: a normal distribution with a mean of 10 and standard deviation of 3 and one with a mean of 25,000 and standard deviation of 5,000. It is easy to see how these two distributions differ (in sheer magnitude, for starters), but what do they have in common? The easy answer is that they are both bell-shaped distributions. The mathematical answer is that there is an equation describing how the probabilities are distributed that differs for the two distributions only in terms of the values for mean and standard deviation that appear as part of the equation. The most practical answer for us, however, is far more powerful: The probability associated with being a certain distance from the mean, measured in units of standard deviation, is the same for both instances of a normal distribution, and indeed for any normal distribution. So all we need to know for a normal distribution is the mean and standard deviation and we can determine the probability of outcomes falling within any range of values.

Consider, for example, our two given normal distributions. One fact that is true for all normal distributions is that the probability of getting an outcome more than one standard deviation less than the mean is approximately 16%. So, for our normal distribution with mean 10 and standard deviation 3, there is a 16% chance we will get a value less than 7 (mean 10 – standard deviation 3). Similarly, though on a completely different scale, there is a 16% chance of getting a value less than 20,000 for our normal distribution with mean 25,000 and standard deviation 5,000 (mean 25,000 – standard deviation 5,000). **Another fact that is true for all normal**

distributions is that there is a 68% (approximate) probability of getting an outcome within one standard deviation of the mean. *For our first distribution, this means a 68% chance of getting a value between 7 and 13 (the mean 10 minus and plus the standard deviation 3) while for the second it means a 68% chance of getting a value between 20,000 and 30,000 (the mean 20,000 minus and plus the standard deviation 5,000).*

We can now return to our question of how to determine if data appear to come from a process that produces a normal distribution. There are three simple facts about normal distributions, one of which has already been mentioned, that are relatively easy to check.

1. **Are half your data above the mean and half below? A normal distribution is symmetrical around the mean.** *(Remember, this is an advantage of a triangular distribution: It does not have to be symmetrical, depending on where you place the most likely value.) If you calculate the mean of the data, and considerably more of the data are on one side of the mean than the other, there is reason to suspect that you do not have a process that produces a normal distribution.*

2. **Are roughly two-thirds of your data within one standard deviation of the mean?** *This check stems from the fact already mentioned: Approximately 68% of the total probability in a normal distribution is assigned to values within one standard deviation of the mean. If you calculate the mean and standard deviation, and the number of data falling within the range, that stretches from one standard deviation below the mean to one standard deviation above, is significantly different from two-thirds, you again probably do not have a process that produces normally distributed outcomes.*

3. **Are approximately 5% of your data more than two standard deviations away from the mean?** *A fact similar to the one above is that approximately 95% of the total probability in a normal distribution is assigned to values within two standard deviations of the mean. Thus, in our first example above, there would be a 95% probability of getting an outcome between 4 and 16, where 4 is two standard deviations below the mean and 16 is two standard deviations above. If significantly more than 5% (or significantly less than 5%, although there may not be many possibilities for being significantly less if you do not have many data) of the data are more than two standard deviations from the mean, you have evidence that the process does not produce a normal distribution. In addition, we can combine the first check with this one to also ask: Are the data that are more than two standard deviations from the mean approximately equally divided between being above the mean and below the mean? (In our example, this would mean that the number of data above 16 is roughly the same as the number below 4.) One significant way in which a normal distribution is not appropriate is if one "tail" of the distribution where tail may be thought of as the part of the distribution more than two standard deviations away from the mean has more probability than the other, or the possible outcomes are stretched out more standard deviations on one side of the mean than the other. When this occurs, the distribution is said to be skewed in the direction of more probability and/or greater deviations from the mean. Assuming a normal distribution under these circumstances can lead to serious errors in analyzing uncertainty, through failing to properly account for the potential to get extreme values on one side of the distribution, but not the other. Excel has a function, NORMDIST, that reports the probability of getting an outcome less than a certain value x for any normal distribution. The function simply requires as parameters the mean and standard deviation of the normal distribution, plus the specification of the value x of interest. The function does this by restating x in terms of how many standard deviations it is away from the mean:*

(x − mean)/(standard deviation)
This is done automatically and is not reported as part of the function's calculation. This value is often referred to as the z value (or zscore or z stat) of x. For example, in our first example, with mean 10 and standard deviation 3, the z-score of 5 would be (5 .− 10)/3 = .−1.67. This can be stated as, "x is 1.67 standard deviations below the mean"
The probability of getting an outcome falling within any range x1 to x2 (where
we assume x1 < x2) can be found by calculating NORMDIST for x2 and subtracting it from NORMDIST for x1. For example, again in our example of mean 10 and standard deviation 3, the NORMDIST value for 7 is .16 and the NORMDIST value for 13 is .84; the probability of being between 7 and 13 is thus .84 -.16 = .68, which is precisely what we said was the probability of getting a value within one standard deviation of the mean in a normal distribution.

In summary, the normal distribution is encountered frequently in practice, but it is by no means ubiquitous. To determine if it is appropriate, you must either understand the underlying process or accept that it satisfies the characteristics of the accumulation process that produces normally distributed outcomes, or check data produced by the process and satisfy yourself that they support the notion of a normal distribution.

Poisson Distribution

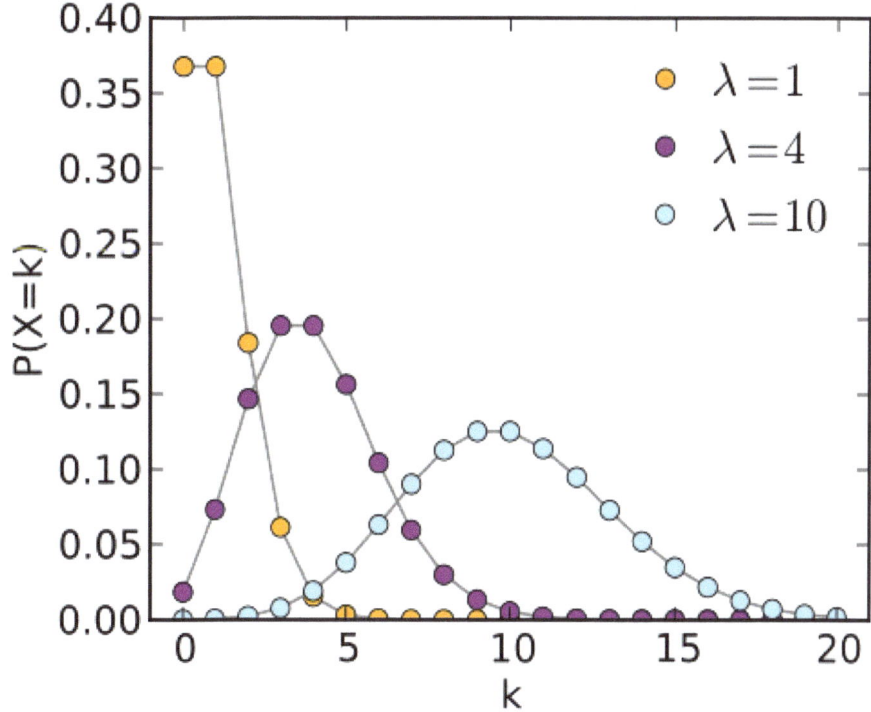

Figure 2: Poisson distribution.

The underlying process that gives rise to the Poisson distribution (unlike the other distributions, "Poisson." is normally capitalized because it is named after the statistician who is credited with first analyzing it, Siméon Denis Poisson, 1781.–1840) is a counting process with an indefinite number of opportunities for an event to occur. Examples of such counting processes include the number of refrigerators sold in a department store in a week, the number of bond issues on the first of December 2004, the number of people that arrive to join an ATM queue between 11:00 and 11:05 am on a given day, or the number of change requests (as defined in PMBOK® Guide) that a project encounters per quarter.

The Poisson is a discrete distribution because we are counting the number of events that occur and the outcome must therefore be a whole number (0, 1, 2, etc.). There are four restrictions on the occurrence of an individual event as part of the underlying process that makes the Poisson distribution appropriate:

1. The probability of an event occurring over any small unit of measure (short period of time, for example) must be proportional to the length of the unit of measure. While thinking of the unit of measure as a period of time such as a day or week is often convenient, other units of measure, such as a page in a newspaper (typographical errors per page) or a roll of sheet metal (blemishes per roll), work as well. Using the time metaphor for unit of measure, another way to state the first restriction is that the probability of an event occurring per unit of time must be constant.

2. Over any unit of measure during which we are counting occurrences, the number of opportunities for the event to occur must be large. A refrigerator sale or a person arriving at the ATM could occur at any instant, for example. Similarly, a blemish on a roll of sheet metal could occur at any point.

3. Even though the probability of an event occurring per unit of measure is constant, the likelihood of two or more events occurring during any particular very small unit of measure must be close to nonexistent (two refrigerator sales cannot occur at precisely the same instant of time).

4. The probability of an event occurring during any particular unit of measure must be independent of what occurs during all other particular units of measure. Using the time metaphor, the probability of an event occurring over the next instant must be independent of whether events occurred in any of the prior instants. In other words, the history of what has already occurred will not affect the probability distribution of the number of future events.

Any process generating the occurrence of events that satisfies these four conditions is known as a Poisson process. When we then count the number of events generated by the process, and the resulting distribution of the number of events during some interval will be a Poisson distribution.

The Poisson distribution, like all the others we have looked at in this note, refers to an
entire family of distributions. The specific distribution is determined by the single parameter λ, the mean number of occurrences per unit of measure. The parameter m is also known as the rate of the Poisson process (for example, on average, 9 people show up at a particular ATM between 11:00 a.m. and 11:05 a.m., so the rate is 9 for this 5-minute interval). The distribution then specifies the probability of having 0, 1, 2, etc., occurrences during any particular interval given that the average number of occurrences per interval is m.

As always, we can appeal to either the underlying process or a check of data to determine if the Poisson distribution is appropriate. One final note to make about this distribution is that if the average number of occurrences per interval is large, the normal distribution gives us a good approximation of the Poisson probabilities. The standard deviation of a Poisson distribution, which does not mean much as long as we are treating it as a Poisson distribution, is equal to the square root of **m**, the mean. Thus, if on average we sell 144 refrigerators per week, we can estimate the probabilities associated with any range of weekly refrigerator sales by using a normal distribution with mean 144 and standard deviation 12, and will get basically the same estimate of probability as if we summed up the Poisson probabilities (with mean 144) for all the whole numbers within the range.

For example, Project X is expected to hit 24 risks in the one-year schedule. Assuming a Poisson risk process, assess the level of risk preparedness required by the project team.

The above Poisson risk process can be approximated by a normal distribution of mean 24 and deviation SQRT(24), assuming the project team is geared to cover risk outages up to the upper limit of 99% risk distribution,

Upper Risk Limit = NORMINV(0.99,24,SQRT[24]) ~35

The team has to be geared toward covering 35 risks during the year (average of ~10 day turn-around per risk), ensuring a 99% risk occurrence coverage in the project.

Also note that, only the mean value was used in the calculation, and the deviation was derived assuming an underlying Poisson process.

Exponential Distribution (Decaying Systems)

The underlying process that generates the exponential distribution is concerned with the occurrence of an event. We are concerned with the time until the next event occurs, and, therefore, the resulting probability distribution of the time until the next event, or waiting time.

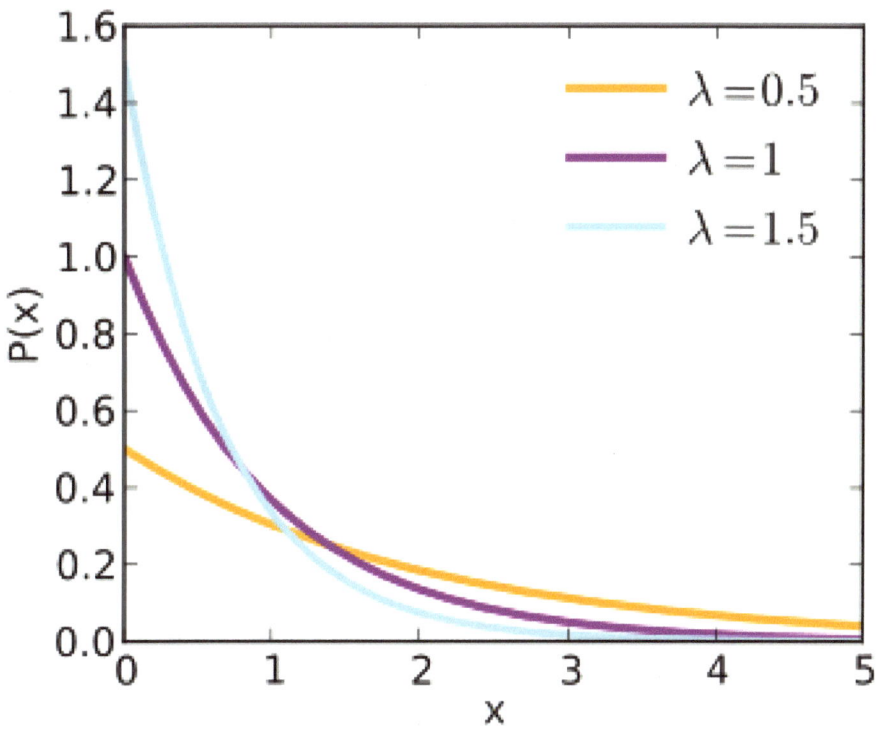

Figure 3: Exponential distribution.

The only condition we need to impose on the event-generating process is as follows. The probability of how much longer it will take until an event occurs cannot depend on how long it has already been since the last event occurred. This condition is known as the memoryless property, because the underlying process does not remember when the last event occurred. Whenever this condition is satisfied, the resulting probability distribution of the time until the next event is the exponential distribution.

The memoryless property is not as restrictive as it may at first appear. Examples of
situations for which the memoryless property, and hence the exponential distribution, have been found to be appropriate include:

- time to failure of most electronic components, such as light bulbs, stereo components, computers, and so forth
- time between arrivals at a service counter, such as a teller window in a bank or a checkout counter in a supermarket
- time until the end of serving a particular customer at a service counter
- time until a project is hit with the next risk

The exponential distribution derives its name because the equation includes the constant "e". This constant can be thought of in the same way as π, which is a critical value in analyzing circles in geometry, and is roughly equal to 3.14. The constant e comes from calculus, where it plays a similarly crucial role, and it is approximately equal to 2.71. In the equation for the exponential distribution, the probabilities associated with values x are found by including x in the exponent of e (the constant e is raised to a power that includes x as part of its calculation); hence the term exponential distribution.

Analytical probability distributions can be extremely useful if and when they apply. They can be used only when the underlying processes satisfy the conditions necessary for their derivation, however, or when you have sufficient data that you are comfortable assuming the distribution fits. When you do not have sufficient data, or cannot understand the underlying process sufficiently, you may want to fall back on simple distributions like the uniform or to represent uncertainty.

Queue Models — An Overview

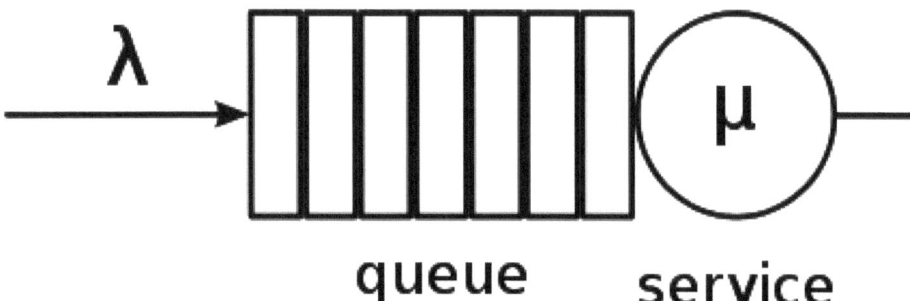

queue   service

Figure 4: Basic M/M/1 Queue Model

We will just touch upon the basic queue model, given the model's relevance to analytically estimate project schedules. We assume we have a single task-processing system and the task arrival is a Poisson process (rate λ). The time taken to complete the task is exponentially distributed (service rate μ); technically, this is an M/M/1 queue model.

The total expected waiting time (queue service) is,

$$T = \frac{1}{\mu - \lambda}$$

Determining the Appropriate Probability Distribution

We must determine which analytical distribution to use for a given problem. There are two major methods we can use: The first method compares the processes that generate the data; the second compares the data distributions themselves. In the first approach, we must define the process that is generating the experienced uncertainty/variation and compare it with those known to generate particular analytical distributions. In the second approach, we generate a frequency distribution from historical data and compare it directly with known analytical probability distributions. The second method is the philosophy behind "best fit" software packages. If we find a significantly close match between our distribution and a particular analytical distribution, we can assume that the underlying process must be of the type that produces that particular analytical distribution, even if we do not have a precise definition of the process itself. It is highly recommended that project and/or program managers use the first method, given that the underlying processes are fairly known or provided in most circumstances.

Analytical probability distributions can be very useful, if and when they apply, and can be used only when the underlying processes satisfy the conditions necessary for their derivation, or when you have sufficient data you are comfortable with, assuming the distribution fits. When you do not have sufficient data, or cannot understand the underlying process sufficiently, you may want to fall back on simple distributions like the uniform distribution to represent uncertainty.

PART 2

Business Analytic Applications

Application of Analytics to Project Management Principles (as described in the PMBOK® Guide)

I used to skip management classes with analytic theory and I just wrote a three-page article on analytic theory! Well, I'm glad I just quantitatively put that statement of pun... Let's begin with real-time analytic application in project management.

Risk Management

Risks in project execution typically arrive at a Poisson process with the inter-risk time exponentially distributed.

For example: The oil & gas exploration industry has matured over the past century. Project data analyses over all initial project launch executions have revealed that these start-up projects encounter an average of approximately six risks within the first year. Ralance Industries, in conjunction with the State Government of Mumbai, has jump-started an oil exploration project in Mumbai's Southern Coast. The project manager of Ralance Industries is faced with the unique challenge of lack of government cooperation in risk management for the next 30 days. What should the project manager recommend to the CEO of Ralance Industries in his or her project status report?

These are real-time situations that global project managers will need to deal with. The project decisions   made today must have strong analytic foundations. An analytical approach with this background is to estimate the chances of Ralance Industries being hit with a risk within the next 30 days.

Using the MS Excel® EXPONDIST formula to calculate the additive/cumulative probability of the occurrence of a risk event in the next one month, where

$P(T <= 30) = EXPONDIST(1/12, 6,1) = 39\%$

The distribution $\lambda(rate)$ is assumed to be 6/year in the above calculation.

The project manager should clearly indicate that the project is subject to an exposure of a 39% chance of being halted due to lack of government support. In practical terms, Ralance Industries may go with a risk of less than 40% against halting the project.

Cost Management

Project cost is a vital piece in today's global project management. Analytics in cost optimization has become more vital because of the uncertainty of global economic equilibrium. Growth geographies face the heat of inflationary forces, while mature markets are being pulled into short-term imbalances of credit investments without underlying dollar generation.

Project management principles (as per the PMBOK® Guide) rightly advocate the principle of lowering project execution costs. Analytics brings in enormous power to this decision-making factor.

Case Study 1

The Philippine government passed the Bio Fuel Act in 2006, and the Agriculture Department was in charge of overseeing its implementation. The law required specific proportions of bio-ethanol to be blended with gasoline. The prime intent was to boost the local production of biofuel feedstock and reduce imports from low-cost production economies (e.g., Brazil). The project management of the bio-ethanol supply chain network for local production was based on highly optimized linear analytic models calculating the production requirements of bio-ethanol in various locations across the Philippines. The complete details are beyond the scope of this article; nonetheless, a basic appreciation of optimization requirements and the importance of project management costing to policymaking is the intent of listing this case.

Case Study 2

The World Health Organization (WHO) has decided to fast track their initiative to reduce the rapid spread of HIV in Kenya. The pilot rollout project aims to reduce spread of the disease and provide treatment to 60% of the infected population. The expected average cost of medication for those under 20 is US$10,000 , US$25,000 for those in the 20-to 35-year-old age group, and US$15,000for those over the age of 35. The National Health Institute of Nairobi has reported that the HIV cases are normally distributed with a mean age of 30 and a standard deviation of 7,and also estimates that there are six million people infected with the disease.

The project plan and budget details have to be submitted for the funding. How does the involved project office calculate the best execution plan and cost of the project?

The statistical information should be leveraged for this case. As per the normal distribution (Figure 5), approximately 68% of the population is covered in one standard deviation from the mean (either side).

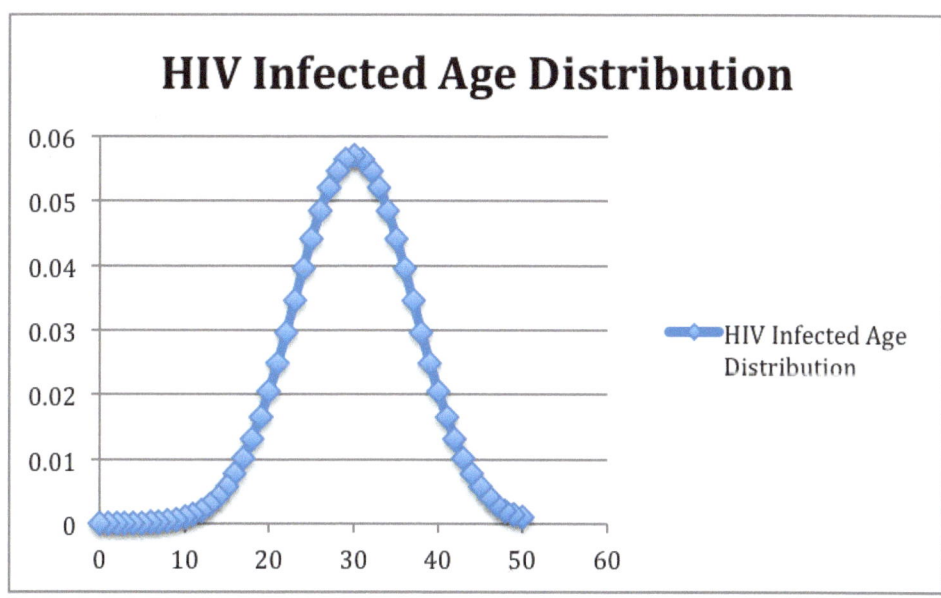

Figure 5: HIV Infected Population Age Distribution

The plot illustrates that approximately 68% of the infected population is between the age group 30 +/−7 (i.e. [23– 37]). This suggests that the project plan should target the age group of 23 to 37 for the initial project rollout. This will ensure that the WHO guideline of 60% is met and the highly dense HIV distribution is targeted.

The project costing has to be split for the age groups [23– 35] and [35+]. The percentage of population covered in this age group can again be calculated from the distribution graph.

Population covered under [23–35] =
NORMDIST(35,30,7,1) - NORMDIST(23,30,7,1)
= 60.4%

Population covered under [35, ∞] =
1 - NORMDIST(35,30,7,1)
= 23.6%

Cost = [25K * 60.4% * 6 M] + [15K * 23.6% * 6 M] =
$US11.2 billion

Schedule Management and Resource Allocation:

One of the challenges faced in maintenance projects is the uncertainty associated with defect inflow from end consumers. Scheduling and budgeting these processes are also prone to high inaccuracies in estimating defect closure rate.

It is worthwhile modeling such projects as an M/M/1 queue to analytical estimate the characteristics of the system like average system response delay to incoming requests or defects. In general decaying system and processes fall under the umbrella_**of Poisson and_Exponential Distributions.**

For example, consider a level 3 software maintenance project that has historically encountered ten defects from the market end customer per month. The arrival rate can be approximated to be a Poisson process with a rate λ = 10/month. The team working on the level 3 project has a collective average throughput of 24 defects per month, which is equivalent to a service rate of μ = 24/month.

Modeling the system as an M/M/1 queue, the average response time of the system is
$1/(\mu - \lambda)$ = $1/(24 - 10)$ = 0.0714 month ~ 2 days. Any defect being logged will take an average of two days for closure.

The project service level agreement should be driven from the calculated response times to ensure customer commitments, in addition to avoid levying any penalty charges to the organization.

Conclusions

I have made a sincere effort to demonstrate the modeling of project management principles to include statistical business analytics to enable projects to execute optimally in all subject areas. By no means do I expect project managers to be statisticians; but a culture of leveraging statistical knowhow to processes can be a key factor these days. I hope the project management principles driven by Project Management Institute will be enhanced over time to add relevant analytics in key project calculations and evaluation procedures.

About the Author

Bharat Gera is a line manager at IBM Corporation. He has been involved in the project management of enterprise software and hardware projects over the past decade and a half. He has worked primarily in storage, database, data warehouse, and analytics domains. He is a Project Management Professional (PMP)® and has an executive management degree with a specialization in business analytics from the Indian Institute of Management, Bangalore. He can be reached at
bharat.gera@alumni.iimb.ernet.in

Disclaimer: The views expressed here are strictly the personal thoughts of the author as deemed applicable to today's Global Project Execution.

Reader Notes

www.ingramcontent.com/pod-product-compliance
Lightning Source LLC
Chambersburg PA
CBHW041111180526
45172CB00001B/211